D1172741

To: ______________________________

From: ______________________________

My heart rejoices and I'm thankful, too,
That I could share this book with you,
For all my poems are woven of
Words I borrow from our Father above . . .
For this is a partnership of three—
God first, then you, and last of all, me—
For I'm not an author writing for fame,
Seeking new laurels or praise for my name—
I am only a worker employed by the Lord,
And great is my gladness and rich my reward
If I can just spread the wonderful story
That God is the answer to eternal glory . . .
And only the people who read my poems
Can help me to reach more hearts and homes,
Bringing new hope and comfort and cheer,
Telling sad hearts there is nothing to fear,
And what greater joy could there be than to share
The love of God and the power of prayer.

THE HELEN STEINER RICE FOUNDATION

God knows no strangers, He loves us all,
The poor, the rich, the great, the small.
He is a Friend who is always there
To share our troubles and lessen our care.
No one is a stranger in God's sight,
For God is love and in His Light
May we, too, try in our small way
To make new friends from day to day.

Whatever the celebration, whatever the day, whatever the event, whatever the occasion, Helen Steiner Rice possessed the ability to express the appropriate feeling for that particular moment in time.

A happening became happier, a sentiment more sentimental, a memory more memorable because of her deep sensitivity to put into understandable language the emotion being experienced. Her positive attitude, her concern for others, and her love of God are identifiable threads woven into her life, her work . . . and even her death.

Prior to her passing, she established the HELEN STEINER RICE FOUNDATION, a nonprofit corporation whose purpose is to award grants to worthy charitable programs that aid the elderly, the needy, and the poor. In her lifetime, these were the individuals about whom Mrs. Rice was greatly concerned.

Royalties from the sale of this book will add to the financial capabilities of the HELEN STEINER RICE FOUNDATION, thus making possible additional grants to various qualified, worthwhile, and charitable programs. Because of her foresight, her caring, and her deep convictions, Helen Steiner Rice continues to touch a countless number of lives. Thank you for your assistance in helping to keep Helen's dream alive.

Virginia J. Ruehlmann, Administrator
The Helen Steiner Rice Foundation
Suite 2100, Atrium Two
221 E. Fourth Street
Cincinnati, Ohio 45201

Helen Steiner Rice

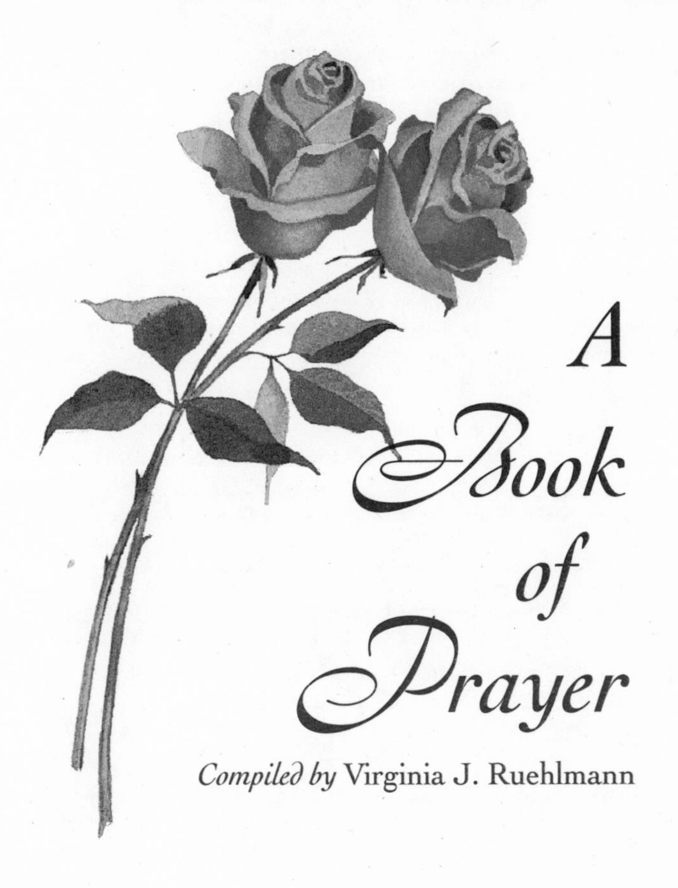

A Book of Prayer

Compiled by Virginia J. Ruehlmann

Published by Fleming H. Revell
a division of Baker Book House Company
P.O. Box 6287, Grand Rapids, MI 49516-6287

Third printing, January 1996

Printed in the United States of America

ISBN 0-8007-1707-4

Jacket and interior illustrations by Jack Brouwer

Dedicated
to all "pray*ers*" of prayers,
especially Hattie R. Decher
whose smile, positive attitude,
words of encouragement
and zest for living
are examples of prayers in action.

Contents

Introduction

Prayer is a magnificent and generous gift from our Father. It is also a conversation, a relationship, a communication with God, initiated by the individual or group doing the praying.

Prayer can be
silent or audible,
spontaneous or formal,
memorized or
extemporaneous,
expressed privately or
with other members of a family,
church, or organization,
said or sung in a secluded location,
or walking on a crowded street,
while driving or riding in a car,
dining or drifting off to sleep.
Anytime and anywhere is a place for prayer.

A prayer can be a form of adoration or praise,
an expression of love and loyalty,
appreciation and thanksgiving,
celebration or consolation, a petition,
a statement of contrition,
a plea for forgiveness or a request for guidance.

Prayers can be simply or elaborately stated.
The important characteristics include
the qualities of humility, fidelity, faith,
trust, and sincerity.
Simple, direct, and honest supplications
are heard as clearly
as loquacious and embellished pontifications.

There are no boundaries as to what to pray for—
one should feel free to take everything
to God in prayer.
The challenge is not only in taking
a concern to Him but
trusting in God's answer and the timing
of His response.

Prayer offers a renewal and revitalization of spirit and hope.
It is not as important to physically kneel
in prayer but rather to have one's spirit
bow in an attitude of respect.

One's prayer life should be an ongoing process,
continuing to become ever more meaningful,
ever more helpful, as
it progresses onward toward the eternal goal.

Helen Steiner Rice knew the value of a consistent prayerful life and expressed such in many of her poems. May this collection assist you in developing and following your own prayer life.

Prayerfully,
Virginia J. Ruehlmann

He was praying in a certain place. When he had finished, one of his disciples asked him, "Lord, teach us to pray, as John taught his disciples."

Luke 11:1 NAB

Helen Steiner Rice writes that "prayer is the uplifting of the heart to God." Catechisms and dictionaries define prayer in a variety of ways ranging from "an offering up of our personal desires to God for things to which He agrees," to "an act of entreating God for certain requests that are important to the one doing the praying." Dwight Eisenhower expressed it this way: "Personal prayer . . . is . . . as basic to the individual as sunshine, food, and water. A thousand experiences have convinced me beyond room of doubt that prayer multiplies the strength of the individual and brings within the scope of his capabilities almost any conceivable objective."

The Meaning of Prayer

Not to Seek, Lord, But to Share

Dear God, much too often
we seek You in prayer
Because we are wallowing
in our own self-despair.
We make every word
we lamentingly speak
An imperative plea
for whatever we seek.
We pray for ourselves
and so seldom for others—
We're concerned with our problems
and not with our brothers.
We seem to forget, Lord,
that the sweet hour of prayer
Is not for self-seeking
but to place in Your care
All the lost souls,
unloved and unknown,
And to keep praying for them
until they're Your own . . .
For it's never enough
to seek God in prayer

With no thought of others
who are lost in despair . . .
So teach us, dear God,
that the power of prayer
Is made stronger by placing
the world in Your care.

And pray in the Spirit on all occasions with all kinds of prayers and requests. With this in mind, be alert and always keep on praying for all the saints.

Ephesians 6:18 NIV

Not What You Want But What God Wills

Do you want what you want when you want it?
Do you pray and expect a reply?
And when it's not instantly answered,
do you feel that God passed you by?
Well, prayers that are prayed in this manner
are really not prayers at all,
For you can't go to God in a hurry
and expect Him to answer your call.
Prayers are not meant for obtaining
what we selfishly wish to acquire,
For God in His wisdom refuses
the things that we wrongly desire . . .
And don't pray for freedom from trouble
or pray that life's trials pass you by.
Instead pray for strength and for courage
to meet life's dark hours and not cry
That God was not there when you called Him
and He turned a deaf ear to your prayer
And just when you needed Him most of all
He left you alone in despair.
Wake up! You are missing completely
the reason and purpose of prayer,

Which is really to keep us contented
  that God holds us safe in His care . . .
And God only answers our pleadings
  when He knows that our wants fill a need,
And whenever our will becomes His will
  there is no prayer that God does not heed.

For this reason, since the day we heard about you, we have not stopped praying for you and asking God to fill you with the knowledge of his will through all spiritual wisdom and understanding.

Colossians 1:9 NIV

No Prayer Goes Unheard

Often we pause and wonder
when we kneel down to pray—
Can God really hear
the prayers that we say?
But if we keep praying
and talking to Him,
He'll brighten the soul
that was clouded and dim—
And as we continue,
our burden seems lighter,
Our sorrow is softened
and our outlook is brighter.
For though we feel helpless
and alone when we start,
A prayer is the key
that opens the heart,
And as the heart opens,
the dear Lord comes in
And the prayer that we felt
we could never begin
Is so easy to say,
for the Lord understands
And He gives us new strength
by the touch of His hands.

What Is Prayer?

Is it measured words that are memorized,
Forcefully said and dramatized,
Offered with pomp and with arrogant pride
In words unmatched to the feelings inside?
No, prayer is so often just words unspoken,
Whispered in tears by a heart that is broken,
For God is already deeply aware
Of the burdens we find too heavy to bear . . .
And all we need do is seek Him in prayer
And without a word He will help us to bear
Our trials and troubles, our sickness and sorrow
And show us the way to a brighter tomorrow.
There's no need at all for impressive prayer,
For the minute we seek God He's already there.

Your Father knows what you need, before you ask Him.
Matthew 6:8 NASB

The prayer of a righteous man is powerful and effective.

James 5:16 NIV

Prayer is powerful. It is one of the strongest forces of energy in the world. It can alter one's outlook: Hatred changes to love, misfortune to blessing, despair to joy, confusion to clarity; ruffled waters become still. Indeed, prayer can change one's life.

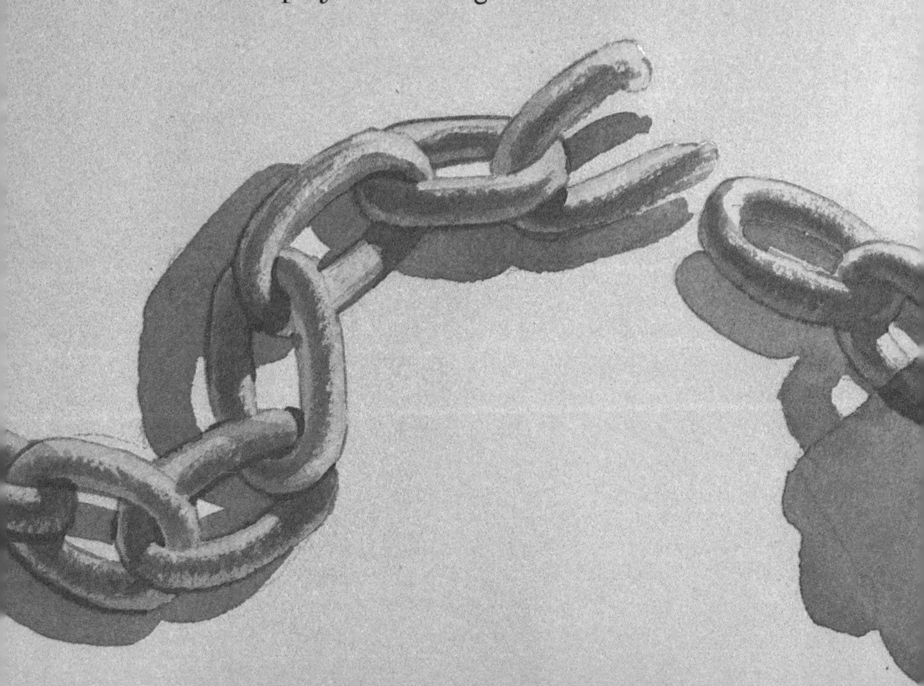

The Power of Prayer

Anywhere Is a Place of Prayer If God Is There

I have prayed on my knees in the morning,
  I have prayed as I walked along,
I have prayed in the silence and darkness,
  and I've prayed to the tune of a song.
I have prayed in the midst of a triumph,
  and I've prayed when I suffered defeat—
I have prayed on the sands of the seashore
  where the waves of the ocean beat.
I have prayed in a velvet, hushed forest
  where the quietness calmed my fears—
I have prayed through suffering and heartache
  when my eyes were blinded with tears.
I have prayed in churches and chapels,
  cathedrals and synagogues, too,
But often I had the feeling
  that my prayers were not getting through.
And I realized then that our Father
  is not really concerned where we pray
Or impressed by our manner of worship
  or the eloquent words that we say.

He is only concerned with our feelings,
and He looks deep into our hearts
And hears the cry of our souls' deep need
that no words could ever impart.
So it isn't the prayer that's expressive
or offered in some special spot—
It's the sincere plea of a sinner,
and God can tell whether or not
We honestly seek His forgiveness
and earnestly mean what we say,
And then and then only God answers
the prayers that we fervently pray.

The Lord has heard my cry for mercy; the Lord accepts my prayer.

Psalm 6:9 NIV

The House of Prayer

Just close your eyes and open your heart
And feel your cares and worries depart.
Just yield yourself to the Father above
And let Him hold you secure in His love.

For life on earth grows more involved
With endless problems that can't be solved,
But God only asks us to do our best—
Then He will take over and finish the rest.

So when you are tired, discouraged and blue,
There's always one door that is opened to you
And that is the door to the house of prayer,
You'll find God waiting to meet you there.

And the house of prayer is no farther away
Than the quiet spot where you kneel and pray,
For the heart is a temple when God is there
As we place ourselves in His loving care.

And He hears every prayer and answers each one
When we pray in His name, "Thy will be done."
And the burdens that seemed too heavy to bear
Are lifted away in the house of prayer.

A Prayer for Healing

I wish I knew some magic words to say
To take your troubles all away,
But at times like this we realize
That God, who is both kind and wise,
Can do what none of us can do,
And that's to heal and comfort you.
So I commend you to His care,
And may He hear your smallest prayer
And grant returning health to you
As only He alone can do.

And the prayer offered in faith will make the sick person well; the Lord will raise him up. If he has sinned, he will be forgiven.

James 5:15 NIV

Prayers Can't Be Answered Unless They Are Prayed

Life without purpose
is barren indeed—
There can't be a harvest
unless you plant seed.
There can't be attainment
unless there's a goal,
And man's but a robot
unless there's a soul.
If we send no ships out,
no ships will come in,
And unless there's a contest,
nobody can win.
For games can't be won
unless they are played
And prayers can't be answered
unless they are prayed.
So whatever is wrong
with your life today,
You'll find a solution
if you kneel down and pray,

Not just for pleasure,
enjoyment and health,
Not just for honors,
prestige and wealth,
But pray for a purpose
to make life worth living,
And pray for the joy
of unselfish giving,
For great is your gladness
and rich your reward
When you make your life's purpose
the choice of the Lord.

On the Wings of Prayer

On the wings of prayer
our burdens take flight
And our load of care
becomes bearably light
And our heavy hearts
are lifted above
To be healed by the balm
of God's wonderful love.
And the tears in our eyes
are dried by the hands
Of a loving Father
who understands
All of our problems,
our fears and despair
When we take them to Him
on the wings of prayer.

But they who wait for the Lord shall renew their strength. They shall mount up with wings like eagles, they shall run and not be weary, they shall walk and not faint.

Isaiah 40:31 RSV

Everyone Needs Someone

People need people
  and friends need friends,
And we all need love,
  for a full life depends
Not on vast riches
  or great acclaim,
Not on success
  or worldly fame,
But on just knowing
  that someone cares
And holds us close
  in their thoughts and prayers.

For only the knowledge
 that we're understood
Makes everyday living
 feel wonderfully good.
And we rob ourselves
 of life's greatest need
When we lock up our hearts
 and fail to heed
The outstretched hand
 reaching to find
A kindred spirit
 whose heart and mind
Are lonely and longing
 to somehow share
Our joys and sorrows
 and to make us aware
That life's completeness
 and richness depends
On the things we share
 with our loved ones and friends.

I constantly remember you in my prayers. Recalling your tears, I long to see you, so that I may be filled with joy.

2 Timothy 1:3–4 NIV

Lives Distressed Cannot Be Blessed

Refuse to be discouraged,
refuse to be distressed,
For when we are despondent,
our lives cannot be blessed.
For doubt and fear and worry
close the door to faith and prayer,
And there's no room for blessings
when we're lost in deep despair.
So remember when you're troubled
with uncertainty and doubt,
It is best to tell our Father
what our fear is all about,
For unless we seek His guidance
when troubled times arise,
We are bound to make decisions
that are twisted and unwise,
But when we view our problems
through the eyes of God above,
Misfortunes turn to blessings
and hatred turns to love.

Let Your Wish Become a Prayer

Put your dearest wish in God's hands today
And discuss it with Him as you faithfully pray,
And you can be sure your wish will come true
If God feels your wish will be good for you . . .
There's no problem too big or question too small—
Just ask God in faith and He'll answer them all—
Not always at once, so be patient and wait,
For God never comes too soon or too late . . .
So trust in His wisdom and believe in His word,
No prayer's unanswered and no prayer's unheard.

If you ask anything in my name, I will do it.
John 14:14 RSV

The Key

Though we feel helpless
  and alone when we start,
A prayer is the key
  that opens the heart,
And as the heart opens,
  the dear Lord comes in
And the prayer that we felt
  we could never begin
Is so easy to say,
  for the Lord understands
And He gives us new strength
  by the touch of His hands.

I pray that out of his glorious riches he may strengthen you with power through his Spirit in your inner being, so that Christ may dwell in your hearts through faith.

Ephesians 3:16–17 NIV

Listen in the Quietness

To try to run away from life
is impossible to do,
For no matter where you chance to go,
your troubles will follow you—
For though the scenery's different,
when you look deep inside you'll find
The same deep, restless longings
that you thought you left behind.
So when life becomes a problem
much too great for us to bear,
Instead of trying to escape,
let us withdraw in prayer—
For withdrawal means renewal
if we withdraw to pray
And listen in the quietness
to hear what God will say.

My soul thirsts for God, for the living God. When can I go and meet with God?

Psalm 42:2 NIV

Give us today our daily bread.

Matthew 6:11 NAB

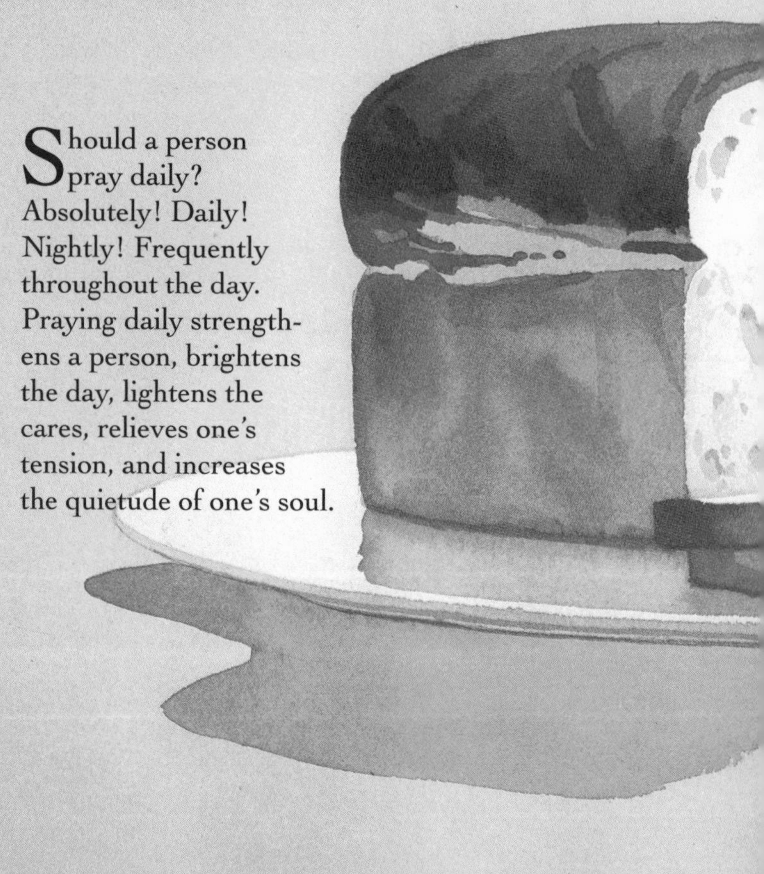

Should a person pray daily? Absolutely! Daily! Nightly! Frequently throughout the day. Praying daily strengthens a person, brightens the day, lightens the cares, relieves one's tension, and increases the quietude of one's soul.

Daily Prayers

The Personal Prayer of the Author

Bless us, heavenly Father—
forgive our erring ways.
Grant us strength to serve Thee,
put purpose in our days.
Give us understanding,
enough to make us kind,
So we may judge all people
with our hearts and not our minds.
And teach us to be patient
in everything we do,
Content to trust Your wisdom
and to follow after You . . .
And help us when we falter
and hear us when we pray,
And receive us in Thy kingdom
to dwell with Thee some day.

This is the prayer that I faithfully say
to help me meet the new dawning day,
For I never could meet life's daily demands
unless I was sure He was holding my hand.
And priceless indeed would be my reward
to know that you shared my prayer to the Lord.

My strength and courage is the LORD,
and he has been my savior.
Psalm 118:14 NAB

Good Morning, God!

You are ushering in another day,
untouched and freshly new,
So here I am to ask You, God,
if You'll renew me, too.
Forgive the many errors
that I made yesterday
And let me try again, dear God,
to walk closer in Thy way.
But, Father, I am well aware
I can't make it on my own,
So take my hand and hold it tight,
for I can't walk alone.

Create in me a pure heart, O God, and renew a steadfast spirit within me.

Psalm 51:10 NIV

My Daily Prayer

God, be my resting place and my protection
In hours of trouble, defeat and dejection.
May I never give way to self-pity and sorrow,
May I always be sure of a better tomorrow,
May I stand undaunted, come what may,
Secure in the knowledge I have only to pray
And ask my Creator and Father above
To keep me serene in His grace and His love!

He who fears the Lord has a secure fortress, and for his children it will be a refuge.

Proverbs 14:26 NIV

Daily Prayers Dissolve Your Cares

I meet God in the morning
and go with Him through the day,
Then in the stillness of the night
before sleep comes I pray
That God will just take over
all the problems I couldn't solve,
And in the peacefulness of sleep
my cares will all dissolve.
So when I open up my eyes
to greet another day,
I'll find myself renewed in strength
and there will open up a way
To meet what seemed impossible
for me to solve alone,
And once again I'll be assured
I am never on my own.

For if we try to stand alone
we are weak and we will fall,
For God is always greatest
when we're helpless, lost and small.
And no day is unmeetable
if, on rising, our first thought
Is to thank God for the blessings
that His loving care has brought.
For there can be no failures
or hopeless, unsaved sinners
If we enlist the help of God,
who makes all losers winners.
So meet Him in the morning
and go with Him through the day,
And thank Him for His guidance
each evening when you pray—
And if you follow faithfully
this daily way to pray,
You will never in your lifetime
face another hopeless day.

My eyes are awake before the watches of the night, that I may meditate upon thy promise.

Psalm 119:148 RSV

It's Me Again, God

Remember me, God?
  I come every day
Just to talk with You, Lord,
  and to learn how to pray.
You make me feel welcome,
  You reach out Your hand.
I need never explain,
  for You understand.
I come to You frightened
  and burdened with care,
So lonely and lost
  and so filled with despair,
And suddenly, Lord,
  I'm no longer afraid—
My burden is lighter
  and the dark shadows fade.
Oh God, what a comfort
  to know that You care
And to know when I seek You,
  You will always be there.

Today's Prayer

Teach me to give of myself
in whatever way I can,
of whatever I have to give.

Teach me to value myself—
my time, my talents,
my purpose, my life,
my meaning in Your world.

Guide me in your truth and teach me; for you are God my Savior.
Psalm 25:5 NIV

The First Thing Every Morning and the Last Thing Every Night

Were you too busy this morning
to quietly stop and pray?
Did you hurry and drink your coffee
then frantically rush away,
Consoling yourself by saying—
God will always be there
Waiting to hear my petitions
ready to answer each prayer?
It's true that the great, generous Savior
forgives our transgressions each day
And patiently waits for lost sheep
who constantly seem to stray,
But moments of prayer once omitted
in the busy rush of the day
Can never again be recaptured,
for they silently slip away.

And no one regains that blessing
that would have been theirs if they'd prayed,
For blessings are lost forever
in prayers that are often delayed.
And strength is gained in the morning
to endure the trials of the day
When we visit with God in person
in a quiet and unhurried way,
For only through prayer that's unhurried
can the needs of the day be met
And only in prayers said at evening
can we sleep without fears or regret—
For all of our errors and failures
that we made in the course of the day
Are freely forgiven at nighttime
when we kneel down and earnestly pray.
So seek the Lord in the morning
and never forget Him at night,
For prayer is an unfailing blessing
that makes every burden seem light.

In the morning, O Lord, you hear my voice; in the morning I lay my requests before you and wait in expectation.

Psalm 5:3 NIV

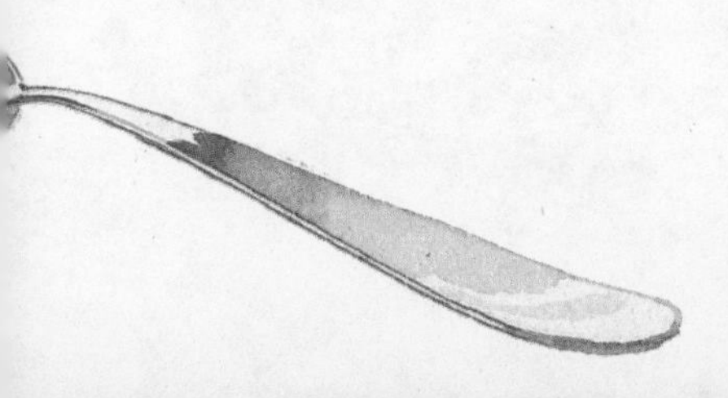

Seek the Lord and his strength, seek his presence continually.

Psalm 105:4 RSV

Often in the quiet and solitude of prayer, a calm and a reverence develop within and God's presence is felt. Equally appreciated are the moments during an act of loving kindness when the presence of God is experienced. Brief, fleeting, but unforgettable, are those seconds when time and the world stand still as the presence of our God is sensed.

God's Presence in Prayer

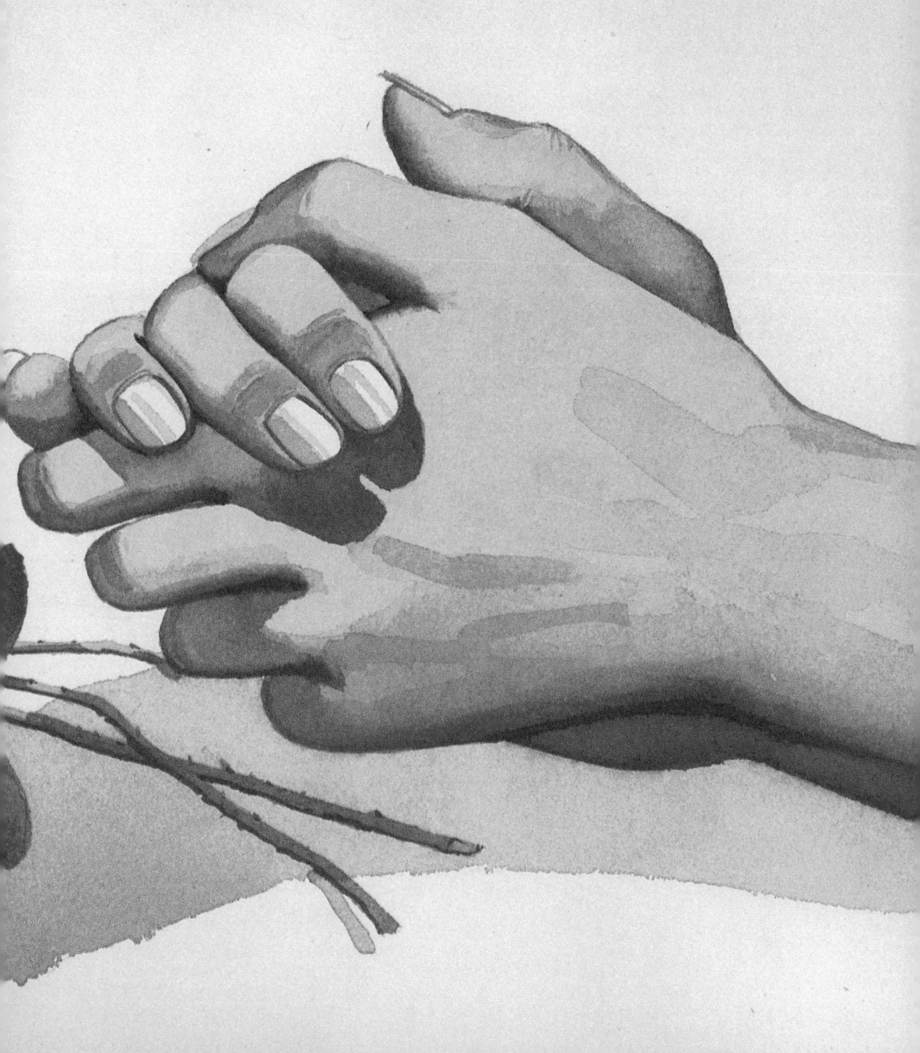

Put Your Problems in God's Hands

Although it sometimes seems to us
our prayers have not been heard,
God always knows our every need
without a single word,
And He will not forsake us
even though the way is steep,
For always He is near to us,
a tender watch to keep.
And in good time He will answer us,
and in His love He'll send
Greater things than we have asked
and blessings without end . . .
So though we do not understand
why trouble comes to man,
Can we not be contented
just to know it is God's plan?

And he said, "My presence will go with you, and I will give you rest."
Exodus 33:14 RSV

The Mystery of Prayer

Beyond that which words can interpret
or theology explain,
The soul feels a shower of refreshment
that falls like the gentle rain
On hearts that are parched with problems
and are searching to find the way
To somehow attract God's attention
through well-chosen words as they pray.
Not knowing that God in His wisdom
can sense all our worry and woe,
For there is nothing we can conceal
that God does not already know.
So if we kneel in prayer in His presence
we'll find no need to speak,
For softly in quiet communion,
God grants us the peace that we seek.

For God alone my soul waits in silence.
Psalm 62:1 RSV

My God Is No Stranger

God is no stranger
  in a faraway place—
He's as close as the wind
  that blows 'cross my face.
It's true I can't see
  the wind as it blows,
But I feel it around me
  and my heart surely knows
That God's mighty hand
  can be felt every minute
For there is nothing on earth
  that God isn't in it—
The sky and the stars,
  the waves and the sea,
The dew on the grass,
  the leaves on a tree
Are constant reminders
  of God and His nearness,
Proclaiming His presence
  with crystal-like clearness—

So how could I think
God was far, far away
When I feel Him beside me
every hour of the day,
And I've plenty of reasons
to know God's my Friend,
And this is one friendship
that time cannot end.

Greater love has no one than this, that he lay down his life for his friends.

John 15:13 NIV

Thy Will Be Done

Only through sorrow
do we grow more aware
That God is our refuge
in times of despair,
For when we are happy
and life's bright and fair,
We often forget
to kneel down in prayer,

But God seems much closer
and needed much more
When trouble and sorrow
stand outside our door,
For then we seek shelter
in His wondrous love,
And we ask Him to send us
help from above.
And that is the reason
we know it is true,
That bright, shining hours
and dark, sad ones, too,
Are part of the plan
God made for each one,
And all we can pray
is "Thy will be done."
And know that you
are never alone,
For God is your Father,
and you're one of His own.

God is our refuge and strength, an ever-present help in trouble. Therefore we will not fear, though the earth give way and the mountains fall into the heart of the sea.

Psalm 46:1–2 NIV

Now I Lay Me Down to Sleep

I remember so well this prayer I said
Each night as my mother tucked me in bed,
And today this same prayer is still the best way
To sign off with God at the end of the day.
And to ask Him your soul to safely keep
As you wearily close your tired eyes in sleep,
Feeling content that the Father above
Will hold you secure in His great arms of love.
And having His promise that if ere you wake
His angels reach down, your sweet soul to take,
Is perfect assurance that, awake or asleep,
God is always right there to tenderly keep
All of His children ever safe in His care,
God's here and He's there and He's everywhere.
So into His hands each night as I sleep
I commend my soul for the dear Lord to keep,
Knowing that if my soul should take flight
It will soar to the land where there is no night.

He will cover you with his feathers, and under his wings you will find refuge; his faithfulness will be your shield and rampart.

Psalm 91:4 NIV

What More Can You Ask?

God's love endureth forever—
 what a wonderful thing to know
When the tides of life run against you
 and your spirit is downcast and low.
God's kindness is ever around you
 always ready to freely impart
Strength to your faltering spirit,
 cheer to your lonely heart.
God's presence is ever beside you,
 as near as the reach of your hand.
You have but to tell Him your troubles—
 there is nothing He won't understand.
And knowing God's love is unfailing,
 and His mercy unending and great,
You have but to trust in His promise—
 God comes not too soon or too late.
So wait with a heart that is patient
 for the goodness of God to prevail,
For never do prayers go unanswered,
 and His mercy and love never fail.

Give thanks to the Lord, for he is good. His love endures forever.
Psalm 136:1 NIV

My Garden of Prayer

My garden beautifies my yard
and adds fragrance to the air,
But it is also my cathedral
and my quiet place of prayer.
So little do we realize
that the glory and the power
Of Him who made the universe
lies hidden in a flower!

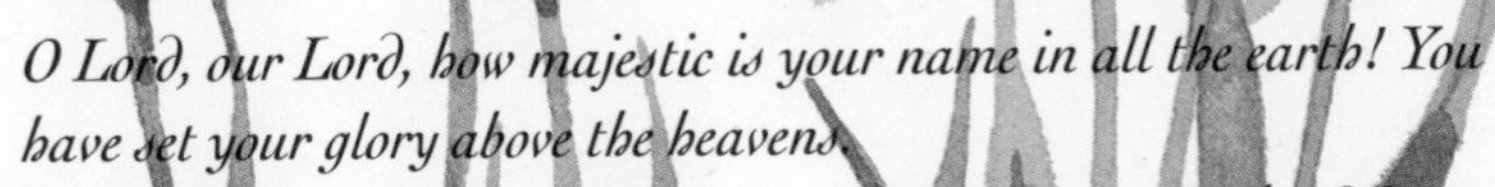

O Lord, our Lord, how majestic is your name in all the earth! You have set your glory above the heavens.

Psalm 8:1 NIV

A Part of Me

Dear God, You are a part of me—
You're all I do and all I see,
You're what I say and what I do,
All my life belongs to You.
You walk with me and talk with me,
For I am Yours eternally,
I cannot dwell apart from You—
You would not ask or want me to,
For You have room within Your heart
To make each child of Yours a part
Of You and all Your love and care
If we but come to You in prayer.

As you have heard from the beginning, his command is that you walk in love.

2 *John* 6 NIV

Enfolded in His Love

The love of God surrounds us
Like the air we breathe around us—
As near as a heartbeat,
As close as a prayer,
And whenever we need Him,
He'll always be there!

The Lord is faithful in all his words, and gracious in all his deeds.
Psalm 145:13 RSV

God, Are You There?

I'm way down here—
You're way up there.
Are You sure You can hear
my faint, faltering prayer?
For I'm so unsure
of just how to pray—
To tell You the truth, God,
I don't know what to say.
I just know I'm lonely
and vaguely disturbed,
Bewildered and restless,
confused and perturbed,
And they tell me that prayer
helps to quiet the mind
And to unburden the heart,
for in stillness we find
A newborn assurance
that Someone does care
And Someone does answer
each small, sincere prayer.

Let us draw near to God with a sincere heart in full assurance of faith.

Hebrews 10:22 NIV

God Bless You and Keep You in His Care

There are many things in life
we cannot understand,
But we must trust God's judgment
and be guided by His hand.
And all who have God's blessing
can rest safely in His care,
For He promises safe passage
on the wings of faith and prayer

By faith Abraham, when called to go to a place he would later receive as his inheritance, obeyed and went, even though he did not know where he was going.

Hebrews 11:8 NIV

To Know

To know beyond belief
that Someone cares
and hears our prayers
provides security for the soul,
peace of mind and joy of heart
that no earthly trials,
tribulations, sickness, or sorrow
can penetrate . . .
For faith makes it wholly possible
to quietly endure
the violent world around us,
for in God we are secure.

The steadfast love of the Lord never ceases, his mercies never come to an end; they are new every morning; great is thy faithfulness.
Lamentations 3:22–23 RSV

For You, a Prayer That God Will Keep You in His Care

Prayers for big and little things
Fly heavenward on angels' wings.
And He who walked by the Galilee
And touched the blind and made them see
And cured the man who long was lame
When he but called God's holy name
Will keep you safely in His care,
And when you need Him, He'll be there.

Then you will call upon me . . . and I will listen to you.
Jeremiah 29:12 NASB

In Hours of Discouragement

Sometimes we feel uncertain
and unsure of everything—
Afraid to make decisions,
dreading what the day will bring.
We keep wishing it were possible
to dispel all fear and doubt
And to understand more readily
just what life is all about.
God has given us the answers,
which too often go unheeded,
But if we search His promises
we'll find everything that's needed
To lift our faltering spirits
and renew our courage, too,

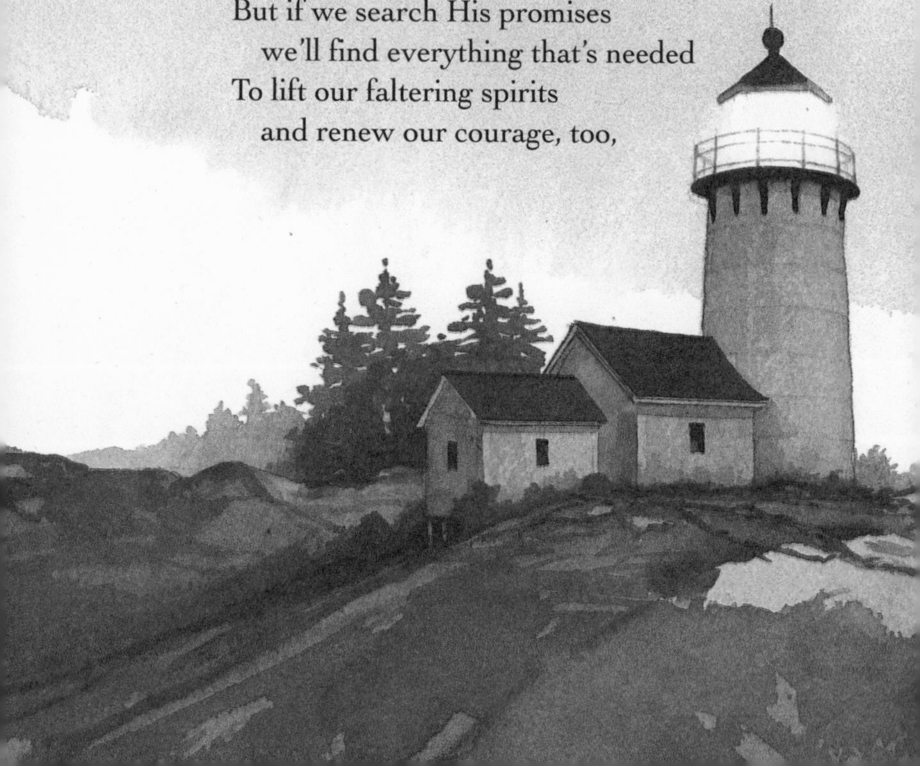

For there's absolutely nothing
  too much for God to do.
For the Lord is our salvation
  and our strength in every fight,
Our redeemer and protector,
  our eternal guiding light.
He has promised to sustain us,
  He's our refuge from all harms,
And underneath this refuge
  are the everlasting arms.
So cast your burden on Him,
  seek His counsel when distressed,
And go to Him for comfort
  when you're lonely and oppressed.
For in God is our encouragement
  in trouble and in trials,
and in suffering and in sorrow
  He will turn our tears to smiles.

The eternal God is your refuge, and underneath are the everlasting arms.

Deuteronomy 33:27 NIV

Love is patient, love is kind.
1 Corinthians 13:4 NAB

It is difficult to suffer uncomplainingly and to bear up under stress when one endures difficult circumstances, insults, or actions. To do this requires the gifts of faith and patience. But the rewards for doing so are contentment and peace. Through prayer we learn to accept life's difficulties with patience.

Patience through Prayer

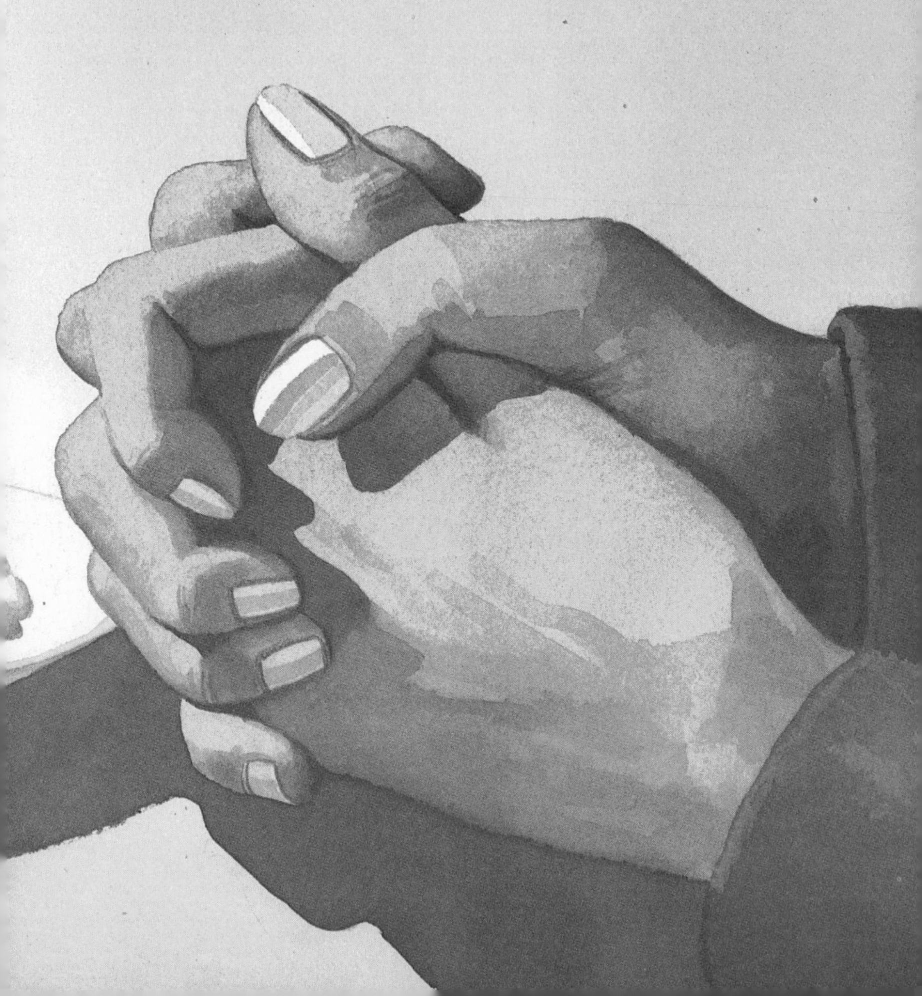

A Prayer for Patience

God, teach me to be patient,
teach me to go slow—
Teach me how to wait on You
when my way I do not know.
Teach me sweet forbearance
when things do not go right
So I remain unruffled
when others grow uptight.
Teach me how to quiet
my racing, rising heart
So I might hear the answer
You are trying to impart.
Teach me to let go, dear God,
and pray undisturbed until
My heart is filled with inner peace
and I learn to know Your will.

Be still before the Lord, and wait patiently for him.
Psalm 37:7 RSV

People's Problems

Everyone has problems in this restless world of care,
Everyone grows weary with the cross they have to bear.
Everyone is troubled and their skies are overcast
As they try to face the future while dwelling in the past.
But people with their problems only listen with one ear,
For people only listen to the things they want to hear,
And only hear the kind of things they're able to believe,
Answers that God gives them they're not ready to receive.

So while the people's problems keep growing every day
And they still try to solve them in their ever willful way,
God seeks to help, and watches, waiting always patiently
To help them solve their problems, whatever they may be.

And he said to all, "If any man would come after me, let him deny himself and take up his cross daily and follow me."

Luke 9:23 RSV

God, Grant Me the Glory of Thy Gift

God, widen my vision so I may see
The afflictions You have sent to me
Not as a cross too heavy to wear
That weighs me down in gloomy despair,
Not as something to hate and despise
But a gift of love sent in disguise—
Something to draw me closer to You,
To teach me patience and forebearance, too,
Something to show me more clearly the way
To serve You and love You more every day,
Something priceless and precious and rare
That will keep me forever safe in Thy care,
Aware of the spiritual strength that is mine
If my selfish, small will is lost in Thine.

For this slight momentary affliction is preparing for us an eternal weight of glory beyond all comparison.

2 Corinthians 4:17 RSV

A Prescription

Just rest with quiet patience
  and seek the Lord in prayer
And place yourself completely
  in His ever-loving care,
Then do not fret or worry—
  God will take good care of you,
For He's the Great Physician
  and there's nothing He can't do.

Look to the Lord and his strength; seek his face always. Remember the wonders he has done, his miracles, and the judgments he pronounced.

1 Chronicles 16:11–12 NIV

Give Me the Contentment of Acceptance

In the deep, dark hours of my distress,
My unworthy life seems a miserable mess.
Handicapped, limited, with my strength decreasing,
The demands on my time keep forever increasing.
And I pray for the flair and the force of youth
So I can keep spreading God's light and His truth,
For my heart's happy hope and my dearest desire
Is to continue to serve You with fervor and fire,
But I no longer have strength to dramatically do
The spectacular things I loved doing for You,
Forgetting entirely that all You required
Was not a servant the world admired
But a humbled heart and a sanctified soul
Whose only mission and purpose and goal
Was to be content with whatever God sends
And to know that to please You really depends
Not on continued and mounting success
But on learning how to become less and less
And to realize that we serve God best
When our one desire and only request

Is not to succumb to worldly acclaim
But to honor ourselves in Your holy name.
So let me say no to the flattery and praise
And quietly spend the rest of my days
Far from the greed and the speed of man,
Who has so distorted God's simple life plan.
And let me be great in the eyes of you, Lord,
For that is the richest, most priceless reward.

The greatest among you will be your servant. For whoever exalts himself will be humbled, and whoever humbles himself will be exalted.

Matthew 23:11–12 NIV

A Special Prayer for You

Oh blessed Father, hear this prayer
And keep all of us in Your care.
Give us patience and inner sight, too,
Just as You often used to do
When on the shores of the Galilee
You touched the blind and they could see
And cured the man who long was lame
When he but called Your holy name.
You are so great, we are so small,
And when trouble comes, as it does to us all,
There's so little that we can do
Except to place our trust in You.
So take the Savior's loving hand
And do not try to understand—
Just let Him lead you where He will,
Through pastures green and waters still,

And place yourself in His loving care,
And He will gladly help you bear
Whatever lies ahead of you,
And God will see you safely through—
And no earthly pain is ever too much
If God bestows His merciful touch.
So I commend you into His care
With a loving thought and a special prayer,
And always remember, whatever betide you,
God is always right beside you,
And you cannot go beyond His love and care,
For we are all a part of God, and God is everywhere.

A Prayer for Patience and Comfort

Realizing my helplessness,
I'm asking God if He will bless
The thoughts you think and all you do
So these dark hours you're passing through
Will lose their grave anxiety
And only deep tranquillity
Will fill your mind and help impart
New strength and courage to your heart.

So place yourself in His loving care
And He will gladly help you bear
Whatever lies ahead of you,
For there is nothing God cannot do.
So I commend you into God's care,
And each day I will say a prayer
That you will feel His presence near
To help dissolve your every fear.

Behold, God is my salvation; I will trust, and will not be afraid, for the Lord God is my strength and my song, and he has become my salvation.

Isaiah 12:2 RSV

Perseverance

Oh Lord, don't let me falter,
don't let me lose my way.
Don't let me cease to carry
my burden, day by day.
Oh Lord, don't let me stumble—
don't let me fall and quit,
Help me to find my task
and help me shoulder it.

You, dear children are from God and have overcome them, because the one who is in you is greater than the one who is in the world.
1 John 4:4 NIV

Anxious Prayers

When we are disturbed with a problem
and our minds are filled with doubt
And we struggle to find a solution
but there seems to be no way out,
We futilely keep on trying
to untangle our web of distress,
But our own little, puny efforts
meet with very little success.
And finally, exhausted and weary,
discouraged and downcast and low,
With no foreseeable answer
and with no other place to go,

We kneel down in sheer desperation
and slowly and stumblingly pray,
Then impatiently wait for an answer,
which we fully expect right away.
And then when God does not answer
in one sudden instant, we say,
"God does not seem to be listening,
so why should we bother to pray?"
But God can't get through to the anxious,
who are much too impatient to wait—
You have to believe in God's promise
that He comes not too soon or too late.
For whether God answers promptly
or delays in answering your prayer,
You must have faith to believe Him
and to know in your heart He'll be there.
So be not impatient or hasty—
just trust in the Lord and believe,
For whatever you ask in faith and love,
in abundance you are sure to receive.

For every one who asks receives . . .
Luke 11:10 RSV

Rejoice always, never cease praying, render constant thanks.
1 Thessalonians 5:16–18 NAB

Every day there are occasions to thank God for the many blessings that He has showered upon us:

the gifts of nature,
the gifts of love,
the gifts of food for our bodies and nourishment for our souls and the greatest gift of all—Jesus Christ, God's Son and the gift of life everlasting.

Prayers of Thanks

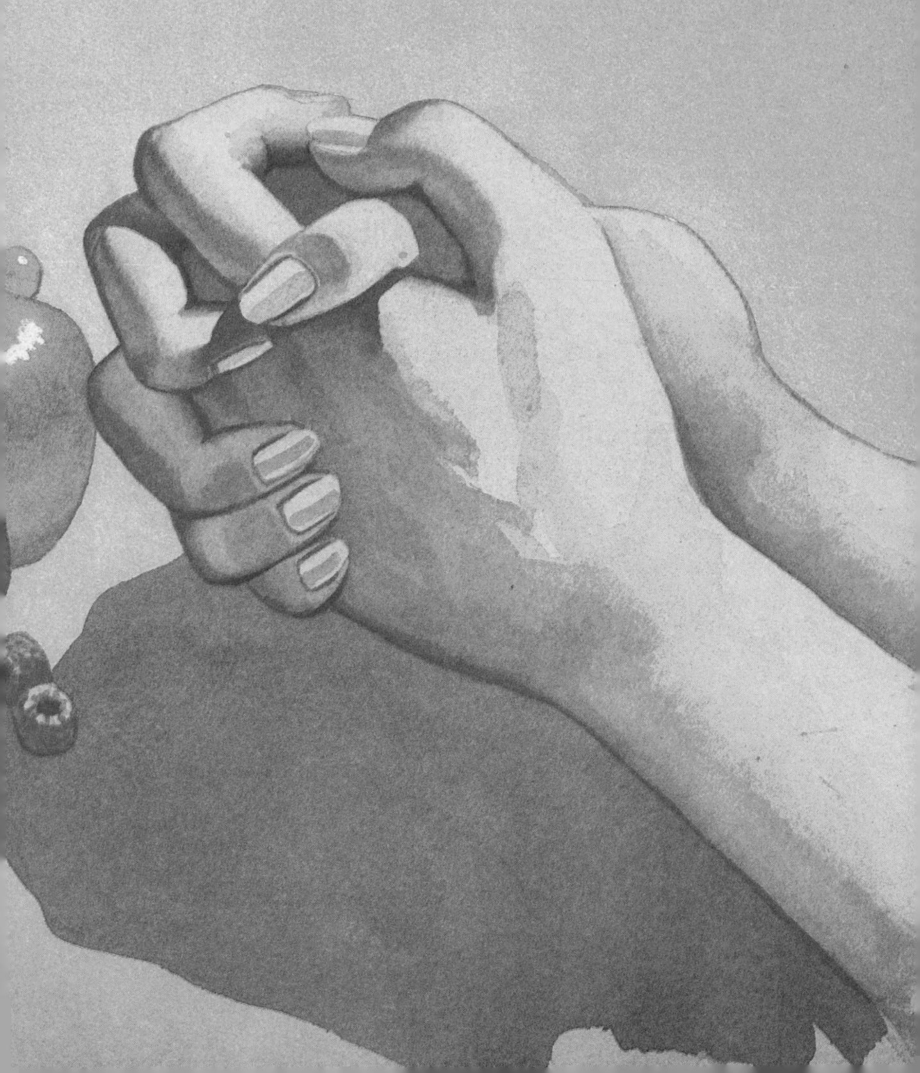

A Thankful Heart

Take nothing for granted,
for whenever you do,
The joy of enjoying
is lessened for you.
For we rob our own lives
much more than we know
When we fail to respond
or in any way show
Our thanks for the blessings
that daily are ours—
The warmth of the sun,
the fragrance of flowers,
The beauty of twilight,
the freshness of dawn,
The coolness of dew
on a green velvet lawn,
The kind little deeds
so thoughtfully done,
The favors of friends
and the love that someone
Unselfishly gives us
in a myriad of ways,
Expecting no payment
and no words of praise.

Oh, great is our loss
  when we no longer find
A thankful response
  to things of this kind.
For the joy of enjoying
  and the fullness of living
Are found in the heart
  that is filled with thanksgiving.

Come into his presence with thanksgiving.
Psalm 95:2 RSV

So Many Reasons to Love the Lord

Thank You, God, for little things
that come unexpectedly
To brighten up a dreary day
that dawned so dismally.
Thank You, God, for brushing
the dark clouds from my mind
And leaving only sunshine
and joy of heart behind.
Oh God, the list is endless
of things to thank You for,
But I take them all for granted
and unconsciously ignore
That everything I think or do,
each movement that I make,
Each measured, rhythmic heartbeat,
each breath of life I take
Is something You have given me
for which there is no way
For me in all my smallness
to in any way repay.

Praise and Thanks to God

Touched by magic colors,
framed by velvet skies,
Nature's lovely masterpiece
serene, enchanting lies . . .
I think this little haven
must be the kind of place
Where very unsuspectingly
we meet God face to face . . .
For God is love and beauty,
and His gifts are peace and rest,
And in His soothing shelter
we are His welcome guests.

Praise the Lord from the heavens, praise him in the heights! Praise him, all his angels, praise him, all his host! Praise him, sun and moon, praise him, all you shining stars!

Psalm 148:1–3 RSV

Thanksgiving Prayer

Thank You, God, for everything—
the big things and the small—
For every good gift comes from You,
the Giver of them all,
And all too often we accept
without any thanks or praise
The gifts You send as blessings
each day in many ways.
And so at this Thanksgiving time
we offer up a prayer
To thank You, God, for giving us
a lot more than our share.
First, thank You for the little things
that often come our way—
The things we take for granted
and don't mention when we pray—
The unexpected courtesy,
the thoughtful, kindly deed,
A hand reached out to help us
in the time of sudden need.
Oh, make us more aware, dear God,
of little daily graces
That come to us with sweet surprise
from never-dreamed-of places.

Then thank You for the miracles
we are much too blind to see,
And give us new awareness
of our many gifts from Thee.
And help us to remember
that the key to life and living
Is to make each prayer a prayer of thanks
and every day Thanksgiving.

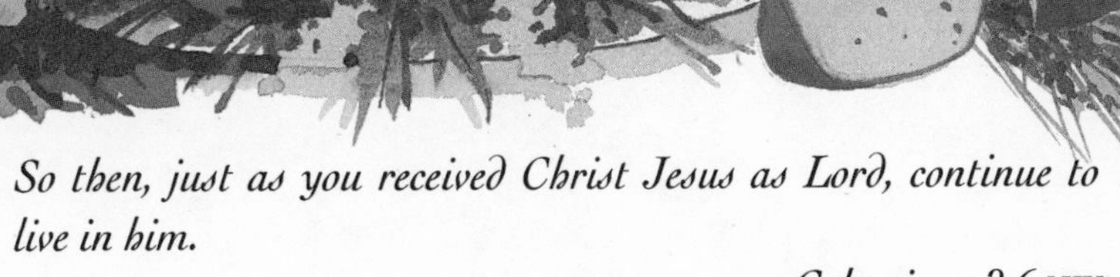

So then, just as you received Christ Jesus as Lord, continue to live in him.

Colossians 2:6 NIV

"Blest too [are] the peacemakers."
Matthew 5:9 NAB

Peace is available to most, but achieved and accepted by too few. The seasons, location, wealth, and nationality are not the deciding factors; peace comes from within and is dependent upon your willingness to forgive, your capability to control bitterness, your ability to trust and to look beyond the present, and your adeptness for encouraging and possessing agape love.

Prayers of Peace

A Prayer for Peace

O God, our help in ages past,
   our hope in years to be,
Look down upon this troubled world
   and see our need of Thee.
For in this age of unrest,
   with violence all around,
We need Thy hand to lead us
   to higher, safer ground.
Without Thy help and counsel
   we are helpless to restore
Safety and security
   in our hearts and homes once more.
And give us strength and courage
   to be honorable and true
And to place our trust implicitly
   in unseen things and You.
And keep us kind and humble
   and fill our hearts with love,
Which in this selfish, greedy world
   man has so little of,
Forgive us our transgressions
   and help us find the way
To a better world of everyone
   where man walks in peace each day.

We Win by Faith

Oh Father, grant once more to men
A simple, childlike faith again,
Forgetting color, race, or creed,
Seeing only the heart's deep need—
For faith alone can save man's soul
And make this torn world once more whole—
And faith in things we cannot see
Requires a child's simplicity.
And there is one unfailing course—
We win by faith and not by force.

"Let the little children come to me, and do not hinder them, for the kingdom of God belongs to such as these. . . . anyone who will not receive the kingdom of God like a little child will never enter it."
Luke 18:16–17 NIV

The Power of Love

There is no thinking person
who can stand untouched today
And view the world around us
drifting downward to decay
Without feeling deep within him
a silent, unnamed dread,
Wondering how to stem the chaos
that lies frighteningly ahead.
But the problems we are facing
cannot humanly be solved,
For our diplomatic strategy
only gets us more involved,
And our skillful ingenuity,
our technology and science
Can never change a sinful heart
filled with hatred and defiance.

So our problems keep on growing
every hour of every day
As we vainly try to solve them
in our own self-willful way,
But man is powerless alone
to clean up the world outside
Until his own polluted soul
is clean and free inside.
For the amazing power of love
is beyond all comprehension,
And it alone can heal this world
of its hatred and dissension.

Be imitators of God, therefore, as dearly loved children and live a life of love, just as Christ loved us and gave himself up for us as a fragrant offering and sacrifice to God.

Ephesians 5:1–2 NIV

Keep Our Nation in Thy Care

We are faced with many problems
that grow bigger day by day,
And as we seek to solve them
in our self-sufficient way,
We keep drifting into chaos,
and our avarice and greed
Blind us to the answer
that would help us meet our need.
Oh God, renew our spirits
and make us more aware

That our future is dependent
on sacrifice and prayer.
Forgive us our transgressions
and revive our faith anew,
So we may all draw closer
to each other and to You.
For when a nation is too proud
to kneel and daily pray,
It will crumble into chaos
and descend into decay.
So stir us with compassion
and raise our standards higher,
And take away our lust for power
and make our one desire
To be a shining symbol
of all that's great and good
As you lead us in our struggle
toward new-found brotherhood.

If my people, who are called by my name, will humble themselves and pray and seek my face and turn from their wicked ways, then will I hear from heaven and will forgive their sin and will heal their land.

2 Chronicles 7:14 NIV

A Prayer in Conclusion

Accept our thanks, Heavenly Father,
For giving meaning to why we pray,
For granting patience as we live
Through each and every day,
For adding power through Your presence
We ask that it never cease.
Help us to be ever grateful
As we strive for inner peace.

V.J.R.